VAHANA

Vehicles of the Gods

STUTI GUPTA

Cuckoo Tales

An imprint of
Srishti Publishers & Distributors

Srishti Publishers & Distributors
A unit of AJR Publishing LLP
212A, Peacock Lane
Shahpur Jat, New Delhi – 110 049
editorial@srishtipublishers.com

First published by
Srishti Publishers & Distributors in 2022

10 9 8 7 6 5 4 3 2 1

The stories have been researched and retold for children, with no intent of hurting anyone's sentiments. The author asserts the moral right to be identified as the author of this work. Images on pages iii, 1, 2, 8, 9, 19, 20, 30, 32, 41, 42, 48, 49, 56, 57, 66, 68, 79, 80, 89, 92, 94, 96, 98 and 100 have been taken from Freepik.com for layout design.

Illustrations by Ishan Trivedi

Dedicated to my Tayaji.

Your 'Buddhu' promises to
Forever uphold the legacy of
Selfless love you have left behind.

Contents

Introduction to the world of gods

Hey Kids!

Let us get started on an amazing journey and read about some of our gods and their mounts. Mounts means... vehicles. Their *vahanas*. Just like you use your bicycles or cars to go from one place to another, the gods also enjoy their rides. But their vehicles are not like ours. They are different.

Before we read some great stories about the vahanas, let us get to know our gods.

The Hindu mythology mentions hundreds of thousands of gods and goddesses. In fact, our sacred books number it at 33 Crores. Can you believe it!

Talking of the gods, the most powerful are the Trinity of gods, the *trimurti*. Brahma, the Creator; Vishnu, the Preserver; and Shiva, the Destroyer. Together, they take care of the world and all life on it. Brahma ji lives in Brahmalok, Vishnu ji's home is called Vaikunth, and Shiv ji's abode is Mount Kailash in the Himalayas.

The other Vedic gods like Indra, Vayu, Varun and several others also have great powers. They are worshipped by a number of people across the world. Indra is the king of gods and his home is called *swarga lok*. The other gods also live there. We will read more about them in the pages to come.

As per popular belief, our world is divided into three parts:

The *swarga lok* or heaven: it is home to the *devas* (gods) and is usually assumed to be above the earth.

The *mrityu lok* or the earth: the world of *manushyas* (human beings) and animals, which we lovingly adore as our home.

The *paataal lok* or the nether world: it is believed to be beneath the earth and home to *asuras* (demons).

Let's read some fun stories about how these gods got their vahana friends. You won't believe some of the adventures they've had together.

What are we waiting for? Let us fasten our seat belts!

Get, set, vroom!

BRAHMA
And his seven swans

Creator of the world

- Born out of a golden egg, though some books mention his birth out of Vishnu's navel on a lotus.

Abode: Brahma lok or Satya lok.

Mount: Swan(s)

Weapons: Brahmastra, Brahmashirsha astra, Brahmanda astra

You can recognize him due to his:

Four heads and four arms; holding the Vedas, a *mala* of prayer beads (*japmala*), a lotus and a *kamandal* (water pot). He sits on a lotus.

Festival: Kartik Purnima

Consort: Saraswati

Finding the perfect mount

When the Trinity of gods decided to create the world and bring life on it, they must have been very thrilled. Think of a startup these days - where founders or co-founders team up to start something new, using the available resources and technology to give life to an idea.

That's exactly what Brahma ji did! He saw the chaos in the universe and put it in order to create this world.[1] He proceeded to create four types of living beings - gods (*devas*), humans (*manushyas*), animals and demons (*asuras*). The three worlds came to be known as *swarga* or heaven for the gods; earth for the humans and animals; and the *paataal lok* or nether world for the demons.

Seems like a cool plan, doesn't it? He started off with a bunch of great ideas, and ensured that nothing went wrong. In fact, he created the world with a lot of love and it was very dear to him.

To look after all his creations, Brahma ji needed to travel between the worlds frequently. He had a lotus flower for a seat, but with all that travel, he realised he would need a vehicle for himself.

Back then there were no fancy cars. Though being

the Creator, he could have created vehicles back then! I wonder why he didn't do that!

So when he felt the need for a vehicle, he decided to choose one of his creations as his *vahana* (mount). That would definitely make travelling easier, wouldn't it?

He knew all the options he had – after all, he had made them! So, he started picking.

Lion? Umm... too violent.

Elephant! Naah. Powerful, but slow.

Parrot? No! Too noisy. I want peace.

Squirrel? Too small!

Horse? I might just fall off. No no... too dangerous!

I need someone who can assist me in my work and understand my mind. Who is impartial like me and has the understanding of right and wrong.

Aha! There is only one such being – pure and perfect for me. A swan!

Children, do you know, a swan is believed to be a wise bird. It is mythically believed that a swan can separate milk from water. I am sure that would be really cool, but it means that the swan has a deep understanding of what is right and what is wrong. In other words, a swan has its heart and mind in the right place.

It glides gracefully so it would be perfect as a vehicle for a journey. Its wings can be my seat belt, Brahma ji thought. And I can hold its neck, if need be. That's decided then!

A swan thus became Brahma ji's vahana.

Pictures of him usually show him sitting on a lotus, with seven swans around him. All of them snowy white, and wise like him. Ready to take him around the world.

There's another god - rather a goddess - whose mount is the swan. Saraswati mata.

She is the goddess of everything related to the power of the mind - knowledge, speech, wisdom, learning, art and all such important things.

I'm sure your mother has asked you to pray to her for wisdom and knowledge. My mumma asks me all the time, and I keep telling my son to seek her blessings!

Saraswati mata is shown wearing a sari, holding a string of beads (*mala*) in one hand, books in the other, and playing a soothing tune on her *veena* (a stringed instrument) with the other two arms. She rides a swan as well, which is a symbol of wisdom and intelligence.

Now that you know how the creator of the world got his vahana, let us go further into the book and read some more fascinating stories.

Fun facts about Brahma Ji:

- Do you know, Brahma ji is shown as having four heads, each looking in the four different directions. His heads also stand for the four Vedas (ancient religious books) – *Rig Veda, Sama Veda, Atharva Veda, Yajur Veda* – and the knowledge that they hold.
- Interestingly, there are not many Brahma temples in the country, though he is one of the most important gods in Hinduism. That is owing to a curse, it is said.
- The most well-known Brahma temple in India is in Pushkar, Rajasthan. Built on the banks of the Pushkar lake, it is a sacred spot visited by thousands of devotees every month.

VISHNU
And his mount - Garuda

Preserver in Hinduism, he takes care of all of Brahma's Creation.

Abode: Vaikunth lok.

Mount: Garuda; Sheshnag
– the thousand-headed snake

Weapons: Sudarshan chakra (discus), Sharanga (bow), Kaumodaki (mace), Nandaka (sword).

You can recognize him due to his:
Reclining on Sheshnag, holding a lotus, Sudarshan chakra, conch shell and mace.

Festivals: All occasions associated with his incarnations (avatars), like Janmashtami, Ram Navmi, Ekadashis, etc.

Consort: Lakshmi

Vishnu sees the brave Garuda

In the holy trinity of gods in Hindu mythology, Vishnu is the preserver. As in, he takes care of the world and whatever happens here. So, like modern day bosses, who send someone to fix a particular problem, Vishnu also takes on an avatar and comes down to the earth to fix any problem. That's how we know of his ten avatars, also known as *dashavataras* in the scriptures.

While we know a lot about his avatars - like Rama, Krishna, Narasimha, Vamana - this story will tell us more about Vishnu ji himself. Trust me, he is as cool as most of his incarnations.

Once it so happened that Vishnu ji was lying comfortably on *Adishesha* - the serpent god. Yes, it is a snake who forever sings praises of Vishnu ji. His other name is Sheshnag.

Now if you're thinking how can someone sleep on a snake, you must remember we are talking of an all-powerful god here. Plus, this snake is the same one that had saved baby Krishna from the terrible rains on the night of his birth.

But coming back to our story, when Vishnu ji was resting on the thousand-headed snake, he heard a sudden noise in heaven. The gods were all running helter-skelter and there were screams all around. Out of curiosity, he peeped in. And what did he see! A huge bird. No, not a bird – a human! Oh, but he had wings. And talons. It was Garuda!

Not long after that, Garuda became Vishnu's mount. Let's read the interesting story of how that happened.

Sage Kashyap had two wives, Vinata and Kadru. Both prayed to sage Kashyap for children. Kadru wanted a thousand snake-kids, while Vinata wanted only two children – equal in power and knowledge. Kashyap granted them their wishes and gave them eggs, out of which children would hatch.

When Vinata's second egg hatched, Garuda was born. He was a grand bird-like human who was so huge that he could block the sun. With a head, beak, wings and talons like an eagle's, he had the body of a human being. He was the king of all birds and very powerful.

In a twist of fate, Vinata had to become Kadru's servant. Garuda couldn't bear to see his mother suffering and asked his serpent step-brothers to set Vinata free. The thousand snakes knew how powerful Garuda was, so they set a near impossible deal with him.

"You will have to get us the amrit that the gods guard in heaven, so that we all can live forever. Then we will set your mother free."

Garuda heard them and was happy that he had a chance to help his mother. He prepared to head to heaven, in order to get the nectar of immortality – the *amrit*. But how would he reach there? He didn't know where heaven was.

He went to his father, sage Kashyap, and asked for directions. Once Kashyap guided him and warned him of all the dangers, Garuda grew himself in size and flew up towards heaven.

He reached the gates of heaven, and was stopped by the sentries. Immediately, an alarm was raised and an entire army of gods appeared, ready to fight him. He realised he needed to be smart to defeat them.

When the army of gods had reached close enough, Garuda flapped his huge wings, raising a storm. The wind was so fierce that it blew away the whole army in different directions. His path was cleared, and he approached the sacred place where the amrit was safely kept.

He saw a cloud of fire above that place, and realised that he would have to cross it to go inside. The fire bubble was hot and could burn him completely. He concentrated and thought of a solution. Then opening his eyes excitedly, he flew down to the earth, filled up his beak and a magical pot with water from the ocean and flew back to heaven. There, he poured all the water on the fire and doused it.

The second challenge crossed, he was closer to the pot of divine nectar. That's when he saw a giant wheel rotating around the pot, which could chop anyone to pieces with its sharp blades. The two sharp blades were rotating really fast and Garuda was stuck thinking how he would cross it!

"Idea! I can also shrink to a small size and slip past the blades," he thought. He smartly reduced himself to the size of an ant and flew from between the blades swiftly. He had just let out a sigh of relief when he saw two huge snakes guarding the pot of amrit.

"I cannot give up now. I have to do this for my mother," he said and went forward.

He turned into his huge form again and raised a storm by flapping his wings. The snakes were thrown off balance with the wind that blew. The snakes landed on the sharp blades of the disk and were instantly chopped into pieces.

He bowed down to the pot of nectar and lifted it respectfully. Then he flew out of heaven to rescue his mother.

He was stopped by Indra on his way back to the earth, but Garuda promised that he would set his mother free and return the amrit to the gods. He wasn't going to give it to the snake step-brothers. Like a true hero, he fulfilled his promise. He rescued his mother, didn't let the snakes misuse the amrit and brought it back to heaven safely.

Vishnu ji had been watching all this from Vaikunth – his home. He noted how bravely and smartly Garuda had carried out his mission. Happy with Garuda's power and intelligence, he offered Garuda the position of his mount.

Garuda was speechless with happiness and agreed at once. Since then, we can see Garuda with Vishnu ji.

Since Garuda had suffered so much due to his cruel step brothers, the snakes, he is also an enemy to all serpents.

The next story will show you how this helped Vishnu ji during one of his avatars on earth.

The snake arrow that hit Rama and Lakshmana

There's one particular story of Garuda that becomes the game changer in Valmiki's *Ramayana*. It tells the story of Rama, who is believed to be an avatar of Vishnu ji on the earth.

Ravana was a very well-read and powerful asura. He was the king of all asuras and everyone was scared of him. When his acts became unbearable for the world, Vishnu ji was born as Rama to rescue the human race.

In the *Ramayana*, Rama's wife Sita was kidnapped by Ravana and kept in Lanka - Ravana's city. Rama, along with his brother Lakshmana and an army of *vanaras* (monkeys) and others challenged Ravana for a battle.

One fateful day during the battle, Ravana's son Indrajit shot a weapon at Rama and Lakshmana. It put them in a deep sleep. The weapon was *nagpash* - or serpent hold. It not only caused Rama and Lakshmana to faint, but also began taking away their breath slowly.

Fearing that the brothers would die with the lethal weapon, the army prayed to Vishnu ji to help. Garuda promptly flew down to the earth once again to save his lord. With his sharp beak and talons, he destroyed the snake charm binding the brothers and set them free.

As the snake charm broke, Rama and Lakshmana were revived and breathed once again. It became a turning point in the battle against Ravana. After this incident, Rama's army went ahead defeating the enemy, and didn't stop till they rescued Sita.

Garuda is an epitome of love and service to Vishnu ji. He is also the symbol of power and wisdom. He arouses fear in those who are guilty, and love in those who devote themselves to good deeds and love.

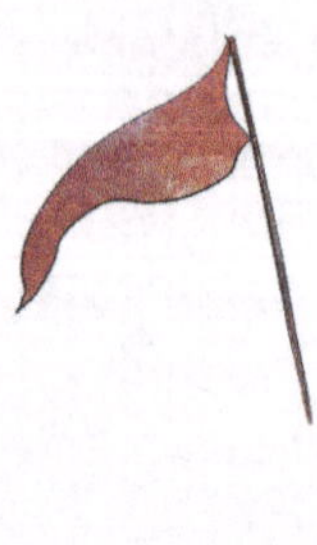

Fun facts about Garuda:

- There is an entire Purana (ancient sacred book) dedicated to Garuda. It is called the *Garuda Purana*.
- A most famous story of Vishnu ji riding Garuda is when they come down to the earth to save Gajendra, the king of elephants, from a crocodile.

SHIVA
And his favourite bull-Nandi

Known as the Destroyer in Hinduism, he eliminates all evil, but also makes way for new beginnings.

Abode: Mount Kailash in the Himalayas.
Mount: Nandi, the bull.
Weapons: Trishul (trident), Pashupat astra, Parashu (axe).
You can recognize him due to:
Ganga river in his hair, snake Vasuki around his neck, crescent moon in his locks, a *damru* (two-headed drum) in his hand.
Festival: Maha Shiv Ratri
Consort: Parvati/ Sati

How Shiva Met Nandi

There was once a sage named Shilad. He was a good man who always helped everyone. Since he did not have a child, another sage told him to worship Indra, the king of gods, for a child.

Well, I should try, he thought.

Happy with his *tapasya* (penance), Indra asked Shilad what he wanted. Shilad requested for a child.

"Oops!" Indra told him that he couldn't grant him that wish. There was only one god in the universe who could give him that kind of a gift – Shiv ji.

Shilad started his tapasya again, focusing his mind and heart on Shiv ji. He was in meditation for so long that his body became just like his surroundings. Anthills came up on his sides and insects ate away his skin. He still did not move!

Don't we all know that Shiv ji is considered to be the easiest to please? He is clean at heart and grants the wishes of all those who worship him sincerely. That's one of the reasons he is called Bhole Nath (a simpleton).

So, Shiv ji was very happy to see Shilad's devotion and appeared before him. When Shilad told him what he wanted, Shiv ji happily granted him the boon. Shilad got back to his *ashram* and performed a *yagna* (a ritual in front of a fire). From the fire was born his son. He named him Nandi - the one who brings happiness and joy.

Nandi was a very intelligent boy. He studied scriptures and became quite knowledgeable by the time he was seven years old. It was then that some sages revealed to Shilad that Nandi did not have long to live. Shilad was heartbroken. Nandi could not bear to see his father sad, so Nandi decided to pray to Shiv ji.

He performed a severe penance on the banks of river Narmada. One fine day, Shiv ji appeared to bless him.

Did you notice how easy it is to make Shiv ji happy? If you think of him with a clear mind and heart, he is pleased.

Anyway, coming back to little Nandi, he was over the moon with happiness when he saw Shiv ji in front of his eyes. He bowed down and asked for just one thing, "Lord, I want to be with you... wherever you are, wherever you go."

"*Tathastu*! So be it," Shiv ji sealed the promise forever. He also gave Nandi a necklace with bells, and offered to take him to the Kailash mountain as his *gana* (follower). That's when Nandi was transformed into half man and half bull. He accompanied Shiv ji to his abode and became his mount – his vahana.

Isn't it amazing how a little boy earned the great place of a god's biggest devotee? He rewrote his destiny. Just like that, if you decide to do something and set your mind and heart on it, you'll be unstoppable.

Nandi does not let Shiva out of his sight

Have you ever been to a Shiva temple? Have you noticed that Shiv ji is worshipped in the form of a *shivalinga*? It is a symbolic representation of Shiv ji. I will tell you about the shivalinga some other time, but for now, let me tell you an interesting story about Nandi and Shiva temples all over the world.

Right opposite every shivalinga, or Shiva statue in any temple, you will find the statue of Nandi, the bull. He always keeps his eyes on Shiv ji and sits right opposite him. Isn't that fascinating! Let us read why.

Once there was a great tug of war between the gods and demons. It was actually not a tug of war, but the churning of the great ocean of milk to receive *amrit* (the nectar for immortality). Anybody who drank even one drop of amrit would never die. So naturally, both gods and demons wanted it desperately. But since neither gods nor demons could do it alone, they decided to team up to get the amrit. *They could always equally divide the amrit in the end,* they thought.

So one fine day, they started churning the ocean of milk, using the snake Vasuki (that we find around Shiv ji's neck) as their rope, and Mandara mountain as the churning rod. But before the nectar came out, there were several other good and not-so-good things that emerged from the ocean.

One was *halahal* – the most dangerous poison ever! All gods and demons started running away to save their lives. The entire universe was in trouble as the poison would kill every being in sight. It was spreading everywhere, and fast!

That is when Shiv ji stepped in to save the day.

Shiv ji drank up all the poison, but did not swallow it. He stored it in his throat, so that it did not kill him. That is the reason why the colour of his neck is blue. The gods and demons thanked him and got back to churning the ocean.

The gods eventually found their amrit, but even after thousands of years had passed, Shiv ji was much troubled by the side effects of the poison in his throat. It caused a burning feeling in his neck and did not let him concentrate.

Every time he sat down to meditate, he wanted something or someone to soothe his burning neck. Back in those days, I am sure they did not have fans or air conditioning, so he looked for someone around him for help.

But who could be with him at all times? Yes, his *vahana* – Nandi!

Nandi happily put himself in Shiv ji's service and kept blowing air on his neck to soothe the burning. Which is why, wherever you see Shiv ji in a meditative pose, you will find Nandi right opposite him. He keeps blowing at the poison stored in Shiv ji's neck, to soothe him of the burning sensation.

So now you know the reason why Nandi sits opposite Shiv ji, not letting the lord out of his sight.

Another fascinating thing about the Nandi statue opposite Shiv ji is also that you have to seek his permission to see Shiv ji. Devotees all over the world believe that since Nandi guards the entrance to all Shiva shrines, they must first offer their prayers to him, and then go to offer their love and prayers to Shiv ji.

Interestingly, it is also believed that he can take your wish to the god faster. That is why it is a popular practice to whisper your wish into Nandi's ears when you go to a Shiva temple.

Just like this, when I was a kid and I wanted my Papa to get me something, I would first tell my Mummy. I knew if she asked him, he'd never say no! It worked so perfectly with my Mummy and Papa, so why not give it a try with Shiv ji and Nandi as well?

***

Fun facts about Nandi:

- The biggest single stone sculpture of Nandi is at the Veerabhadra temple at Lepakshi, Andhra Pradesh.
- Nandi is believed to play the *mridanga* (an elongated drum like musical instrument) very well.
- The first visual of Nandi and Shiva was seen on the Pashupati seal from the ancient Indus Valley Civilisation.
- Nandi is the head of all Shiv ji's ganas.

Ganesh ji and his mouse are having a feast! Do you want to add some colour to their celebration?

DURGA
And the ferocious lion - Dawon

- Born with the combined powers of the trinity of gods, Durga is a warrior goddess.
- She is worshipped as a loving mother, who can take a fierce form to save her devotees.

Mount: Lion named Dawon

Weapons: Chakra (discus), Shankha (conch shell), Gada (mace), Trishul (trident), Khanda (sword), Ghanta (bell)

You can recognize her by:

Dressed in red, seated majestically on a lion, her ten arms holding up ten weapons.

Festivals: Navaratri, Durga Puja, Durga Ashtami, Vijaya Dashami

How Maa Durga Came to be

Maa Durga is known as the fierce battle goddess on the one hand, and on the other, she is worshipped as the loving mother who takes care of her devotees. But there is an interesting story on how she came to be, and how the mighty king of the jungle, a lion, became her mount. Let's read more to find out.

You know, as a child, I was always amused when I saw the beautiful goddess sitting on a lion. I also remember asking my parents to get me a lion as a pet so that I could also go to school on it. My parents laughed it away then, but now I know how silly that request must have sounded.

Long time ago, the demon king Rambha was infamous for upsetting all the good people on earth. His wife, Queen Shyamala was part demon, part water buffalo. So when they were blessed with a son, they were quite excited. They named him Mahishasur.

Mahishasur grew up to be a powerful demon himself, and prayed to Brahma ji for a boon. Like all the others, he also wanted the boon of immortality so that he could live forever. But he also knew that none of the gods would grant him that boon so easily. So, he twisted the demand a little. He asked Brahma ji to bless him so that he couldn't be killed by any god, demon, man or animal. He was sure everyone else remaining would be weak enough for him to defeat.

He performed tapasya sincerely and earned the desired boon from Brahma ji. Now that he knew he was undefeatable, he went crazy by breaking ashrams, destroying cities and homes, annoying people, not letting them pray, and also going and creating chaos in the city of gods! He was a master of stealth, so he kept changing his form and finding new ways to irritate people on the earth as well as in heaven.

All the gods and humans were fed up of Mahishasur and didn't know how to stop him. So the humans prayed to the gods, and the gods prayed to the super gods – Brahma ji, Shiv ji and Vishnu ji.

The gods were upset with Brahma ji for granting the demon such a boon. Now how would they find someone who was not a god, demon, animal or human to kill Mahishasur? It seemed like an impossible task.

That's when the Tridev closed their eyes. A strange divine light could be seen around them, as if there was some energy flowing out of the three. Then the three energies came together and started forming a shape.

What was it?

Some weapon? No no!

Some thought it was an animal. No, it looked too beautiful.

Oh god, it was a woman! A beautiful one with almond-shaped eyes, long and curly hair, and an amazing halo around her.

That is how Goddess Durga was born. When the rest of the gods saw her, they gave her some weapons to help her fight Mahishasur. Shiv ji gave her the trishul, Vishnu ji gave her his chakra, Brahma ji gave her a pot full of sacred water, etc.

Finally, she was ready to fight Mahishasur. Since his boon never said 'woman', this became the only way for the gods to defeat him.

But how would she reach the demon? The Himalaya mountains were watching her preparations, so the mountain gave her a grand lion to serve as her vahana. She sat on the lion named Dawon and headed towards Mahishasur.

She reached his kingdom and shouted his name to call him out. When Mahishasur saw a woman on a lion, he was a little confused. He sent his army to fight the woman, but one after the other, all his men were killed mercilessly. Now he knew this was no ordinary woman and prepared for battle.

The battle went on for nine days. Since Mahishasur could change into any form at will, he kept changing into various animals and confusing Maa Durga.

On the tenth day, there came a point when Maa Durga pinned him down, and just as he was changing into a buffalo, she thrust the trishul into his chest, killing him.

With Mahishasur's death, all the gods showered flowers on Maa Durga and rejoiced. The demon was dead and they were free again.

From that day on, Maa Durga is worshipped as the benevolent mother who saved the world, and also the warrior goddess who can kill to save her devotees.

A strange encounter

Shiv ji is known as the god of gods, Mahadev. He is mostly seen in a meditative pose, and is also worshipped as a yogi himself. Once it so happened, that Shiv ji's tapasya went on for a really long time. So long that Parvati was tired of waiting for him. She decided to sit in meditation as well and wait for her husband.

She was meditating for many hundreds of years, not worrying about the sun, heat, rain or winter chills. The weather took its toll on her body and her beautiful skin became tanned and dark.

When she opened her eyes, she knew in her heart that Shiv ji was back on Kailash mountain after finishing his tapasya. She also promptly returned to reunite with him. They both were glad to see each other after such a long time, and began chatting.

While joking about something, Shiv ji told Parvati mata how she had become very dark. He even said, "You look more like Kali than Parvati today."

His words upset Parvati mata. And why wouldn't they? After all, she had waited for Shiv ji for so long. She couldn't imagine why he would make fun of her! Anyway, body shaming is not cool. We cannot, and must not make fun of anyone for their body type, complexion, or anything at all. Everyone is special, and Shiv ji had forgotten this important lesson.

Parvati mata was so angry that she left for the forest, and sat in tapasya again to calm herself down. While she had been sitting in penance, a hungry lion came towards her. Seeing her, he was happy to have found something to eat.

However, as he came closer, he found that the beautiful goddess was in meditation. The lion didn't want to disturb her, so it sat there for years, waiting for Parvati mata to finish her tapasya.

He looked at her so dedicatedly, that he forgot all about his food and water. In a way, he was also meditating along with her.

When Parvati mata opened her eyes, she saw the lion sitting in front of her, looking straight at her. She had a *divya drishti* (divine vision) which told her that this lion had come to eat her. But now, he had become her *bhakta* or devotee because of the meditation.

So, she took him back to Kailash mountain with her and made him her mount. Hence, though there are many forms of the goddess, her mount is always the same – the lion.

Fun facts about Maa Durga:

- There is a popular trend of Kumari Puja or Kanjak in many parts of the country, where young girls are adored as a form of goddess Durga.
- There are nine forms of Durga, known as the Nava-durga, worshipped during the festival of Navaratri.
- Unlike the other representations of goddesses, Durga maa is a balanced rendering of a warrior goddess and a loving mother.

LAKSHMI
And her dear owl-Uluka

- Believed to be the daughter of divine sage Bhrigu and his wife Khyati.
- She is worshipped as the goddess that gives wealth and riches.

Mount: Owl

You can recognize her due to:

Seated on a lotus, she is holding a Shankha (conch), Padma (lotus), Gada (mace) and gold coins.

Festivals: Diwali, Varalakshmi vrata, Navaratri.

Consort: Vishnu

Finding the perfect match

When Brahma ji created the universe, the gods loved the plants, animals, stars and water bodies. But most of all, they loved us humans. It is said that Brahma ji created us all in the form of gods, just minus the super powers.

What fun it would have been to have those powers! But to compensate, he gave us our mind and the motivation to be special.

So obviously, the gods loved visiting the earth from their abode in swarga, sometimes to meet humans to grant them boons for their penance, or just for a break from the usual workings of god-life.

The constant travel to and from earth made them really tired. They realised the need for a vahana and began their search for one. Remember, how Brahma ji had been looking for one too? Similarly, some gods and goddesses went to the earth to find their perfect match. Lakshmi ji was one of them.

She was a busy goddess – in charge of giving people wealth and prosperity. As humans began to understand the world better, their thirst for wealth also increased. So Lakshmi ji ended up coming down to earth very frequently, sometimes in the dead of the night too.

She got talking to some of her fellow gods, who advised her to go to earth and find a suitable mount. So she did!

When she landed in the midst of a forest, the sun was shining brightly. She knew that a forest was where most animals lived, and she was right! Lakshmi ji was soon surrounded by birds and animals of all kinds. Squirrels and monkeys, hippos and hyenas, eagles and owls – all gathered beside her.

They all looked at her so hopefully that she was confused about who she should pick. She had to find a way.

She began to ponder when a brilliant idea struck her. It was indeed a smart idea!

"Thank you so much for coming over to help me. I am deeply touched by your love. But I must pick only one, and the most suitable. I think we should have a race."

The animals and birds agreed. "We shall all assemble at one spot, and then all of you will have to find me. Whoever reaches me first, shall be my vahana."

Fair enough! Everyone started getting ready for the race.

By the time they reached the starting line, it was dusk. The sun was setting and it would soon be dark. Some of the animals were not comfortable with the dark, but how could they let this opportunity pass? So the race finally began!

All the participants used their senses of smell and sight

and tried to find Lakshmi ji. The goddess patiently waited by the riverside, excited about finding her new mount.

After a long wait, she saw the owl approaching her. His name was Uluka[2] . He told Lakshmi ji how he could see clearly in the dark too and had a mighty good sense of judgment.

Lakshmi ji heard him and waited for all other animals and birds to reach her. When they had gathered again, she announced.

"Since Uluka the owl has won the race, he will be my vahana!"

Uluka hooted in delight! But the others were silent.

After a brief silence, they all protested that it wasn't a fair game.

"Lakshmi ji! I couldn't even see where I had to go. It is a moonless night, pitch dark!" screamed the parrot, obviously unhappy about losing the race.

Lakshmi ji smiled and told them all, "That was just perfect, actually. My devotees worship me on *amavasya*, a moonless night of the Kartik month. You know, they call it Diwali. So I have to go to their houses on Diwali, and I need someone who is comfortable in the dark. I think Uluka will be perfect."

Uluka bent forth and offered his pranam to Lakshmi ji. She hopped onto his back and off they flew towards swarga lok.

---

2 Sanskrit for owl.

Generally, an owl is considered to be a wise bird. With a fair sense of judgment, it is one of the smartest. His accompanying the goddess of wealth and prosperity only goes to show that she always has a wise one to fall back on - literally.

Fun facts about Lakshmi Ji and Uluka:

- Every time Vishnu ji incarnates on the earth, Lakshmi ji takes birth as his partner.
- There are eight manifestations of Lakshmi, called the Ashta-Lakshmi.
- Uluka is best known for being unwavering in his decisions.
- The symbol of owl is believed to help achieve wealth and success.

MAA SHASHTHI
And her beloved cat

- Born to Indra and Sachi, she is the goddess of fertility.
- She is worshipped for maintaining the health and wellness of children.

Mount: Cat

You can recognize her due to:

Seated on a lotus, she is surrounded by children. She also has a cat near her.

Festivals: Durga Puja, Nag Panchami.

Consort: Kartikeya (identified with Devasena)

Who stole the food?

Indian ancient texts are full of stories. And a very important part of these stories are the *vrat kathas.* They are basically those stories that people read out or narrate on fasting days.

The story you are about to read is also very popular. It is about Goddess Shashthi[3] who is considered to be a loving goddess, who takes care of children and watches over them. Shashthi pujan is a grand affair during the Navaratri[4] festival where she is venerated on the sixth day.

It is believed that she is the giver of children and also their protector. She is always shown with one or more infants in her lap, and with her beloved vahana, a black cat, sitting near her.

There is an interesting story about the cat that also includes a tale about how the goddess teaches a lesson to a proud young woman[5].

---

3 Also called Shashti, literally meaning sixth.

4 Festival that goes on for nine days, celebrated to mark the victory of Maa Durga over Mahishasur.

5 Jamai Shahshti vrat katha. Also a Bengali folk tale.

Once upon a time, in a wealthy household, a farmer lived with his wife and seven sons. They were a happy family who lived in harmony. They had a huge house, a pond with big fish, and several fields which yielded good crop. The farmer was content as all his sons were married to women from respectable families. All in all, it seemed like the perfect family.

The youngest daughter-in-law in the house (who everyone called Chhoto-bou) was a little different from the others. She was rather fond of eating, almost to a fault. It wasn't as though she ate a little more than the others, she overate quite a lot. You could call her a glutton, because once she set her eyes on something, she couldn't stop eating. And fish was her absolute favourite!

Everyone in the house ate together, as a family. The cooks would prepare the meal, set it in the kitchen, and serve it at the meal time. Once when the family was sitting together and eating, there was not enough fish for everyone. The head of the family, the father, asked the cook angrily, "Why did you not make enough fish for everyone? Is there a shortage in our pond?"

The cook didn't say anything; he was too scared to even breathe a word.

Slowly, everyone in the house started noticing that food kept vanishing – especially milk, sweets and fish!

The farmer's wife summoned everyone and asked, "There's food being stolen from the kitchen. Who is the culprit? Tell me!" she roared.

Everyone was too confused and didn't really know what was happening. Nobody knew that it was Chhoto-bou who entered the kitchen unnoticed, eating up the sweets, drinking up all the milk and stealing the fish!

But to save herself, Chhoto-bou quickly said, "Maa, I have often seen a black cat going into the kitchen. I think it was her..."

That was it! The fate of the cat was sealed with that lie.

When Shashthi maa's favourite black cat ambled into the house the next morning, the house helps and cook caught her and beat her. She ran away, sad and hurt.

This was repeated almost every other day. Chhoto-bou would steal the food, blame the cat and the cat would be beaten up.

Upset with the treatment she was getting, the cat went to her beloved Shashthi maa and told her everything. She sobbed and cried and didn't know how to set things right.

Shashthi mata was very angry when she learned that a human being was lying and causing hurt to a mere animal, for her personal gain. She decided to teach Chhoto-bou a lesson. She instructed the cat to not go into that house till the right time came.

Several months later, Chhoto-bou gave birth to a child. There were celebrations in the family. But then, one night, the child went missing. They looked everywhere, but couldn't find the child anywhere. Chhoto-bou was inconsolable, unable to understand who would do this to her.

Many miles away, the cat handed over the wailing child to Shashthi mata, putting the baby in her tender care.

The next year, Chhoto-bou had another baby, and the cat came to the house that night as well. Chhoto-bou saw the cat running away with the baby. She quickly removed her bangle and threw it at the cat. It hit the cat, causing it to bleed.

Chhoto-bou followed the trail of blood and reached Shashthi mata. When she saw both her children in the lap of the goddess, she was relieved. Then she saw the cat sitting lovingly by the goddess's feet and complained, "Maa, this horrible cat has been stealing my children. Please punish her."

Shashthi mata told her angrily, "This cat is my beloved child. My vahana! How dare you blame her of your petty thefts and harm her! You have caused harm to my child, and that is why your children are away from you."

Chhoto-bou cried and cried, apologising that she had made the biggest mistake of her life by telling lies. She promised to mend her ways and confess the truth to everyone in the family. She also touched the cat's feet. The cat felt bad for her and forgave her.

Chhoto-bou returned to her house and told everyone the truth. She became a devotee of Shashthi mata, and wholeheartedly observed a fast and offered prayers to her every year.

Who would have thought stealing food would lead to this essential lesson for the Chhoto-bou! This story is so simple, yet so powerful. Isn't it?

Can you find the perfect match here?

INDRA
And his majestic elephant – Airavat

- King of gods.
- Born to sage Kashyap and Aditi.

Abode: Indra lok in Swarga.

Mount: Airavat, the elephant

Weapons: Vajra (thunderbolt), Indra astra

You can recognize him due to:

Carries a thunderbolt shaped weapon, and is seen with his mount Airavat.

Festival: Indra Jatra, Sawan

Consort: Shachi

Lord Brahma gives Indra his Mount

By now, you have come across the name Indra many times. And I am sure you also know that Indra is worshipped as the king of all devas. He enjoys much power in the world and is worshipped as the deity that brings rains.

Airavat is a majestic white elephant with four tusks and seven trunks. He wears charming golden rings in his tusks and looks rather cool. He is the king of elephants and thus the apt vehicle for the king of gods.

But Indra did not have Airavat with him all the time. There had been days when he had been looking for a vahana fit for him, and wasn't able to find any.

Sad and confused, he went to Brahma ji, the creator of this universe. Let's see what happened next.

Brahma ji was sitting on his lotus, meditating on his creations. He just had to close his eyes and focus, and he could see what was happening in any part of the world – whether it be the earth, heaven or the nether world. Isn't that cool? It's like having a CCTV camera inside your head.

But never mind that. He could see Indra approaching him, looking rather grim and disappointed.

He opened his eyes just as Indra reached before him and asked him, "Why do you look so sad, young man?"

"I am just a few thousand years old, Brahma ji. Not too old." They laughed softly. Then Indra became sad again as he said. "I had to walk all the way to come here. I am so tired of going on my travels on my own. I need a vahana and I cannot find a befitting one anywhere. Please help me, Brahma ji!"

Brahma ji smiled and said, "Alright, alright. Stop complaining! Come back tomorrow and I shall give you your mount. Be here at the same time!"

Indra instantly forgot all his tiredness and disappointment. He clapped his hands in glee and turned around to walk back to heaven. He was very excited, wondering what his vahana would be!

In the meantime, Brahma ji went to Vishnu and requested to see Garuda, Vishnu ji's mount. Garuda humbly joined his hands and offered his service.

You have read the story of Garuda's birth and know already that he came out of an egg. Brahma ji asked Garuda to get him the broken shells of the same egg that he was born out of. Garuda didn't really understand why, so he looked sideways at Vishnu ji and caught him smiling. He decided to go ahead and get the shells. After all, he couldn't question the Creator of the whole world, could he?

Once Brahma ji had the shells, he focused all his attention on them and chanted some sacred mantras. As his voice rose, the intensity of the chanting also became stronger. A few seconds later, the shells began to shake and tremble. Lo and behold! What was coming out? It looked like something huge. An elephant!

Garuda couldn't believe his eyes and stared at the majestic elephant emerging out of the shells. The snow-white elephant was shining in splendour. He had golden rings on his tusks. Oh, it had four tusks, not two. And just as they all saw his trunk emerge, they felt there was something behind it. Oh another trunk... and another... and another! This was no ordinary elephant for sure.

By the time the white elephant stood outside of the shells, Garuda was completely awed. Brahma ji named this elephant with seven trunks and four tusks, Airavat. He knew that this king of elephants would be a fitting vahana for the king of gods.

The next day, when Indra came to see Brahma ji, he looked tired but excited. He couldn't wait to see his new vehicle. When he set his eyes on Airavat, he jumped in happiness. This was just perfect!

Since that day to this day, nobody has ever seen Indra without his beloved Airavat.

Not just regal in physical form, Airavat also holds the wisdom of the scriptures. He his with Indra day and night, like his shadow, and also guards the gates to swarga lok.

When the god of rain wanted help

One fine morning, the sun was shining brightly on the earth. A little too brightly. Indra sat sad-faced, looking down at several people performing a puja. Airavat was looking after the security operations at the gate to heaven. They were going to have a good feast today.

When Airavat looked at Indra's downcast face, he couldn't understand why the king of gods was so unhappy. He went to ask Indra what the matter was.

Indra said sadly, "I am waiting to bring down some rain."

"That's wonderful! Why are you sad then?" Airavat asked, unable to understand.

Indra showed the humans performing the puja on the earth and told Airavat that all those farmers were praying to him. He wanted to help them, but didn't know how.

Indra explained that on the earth, people depended on rivers, oceans and lakes for water. While all these water sources were rich, he wanted to find a way to give humans the blessing of rains. He wanted them to feel this nectar dropping down on them like blessings from the heavens above.

Airavat thought for a bit and offered to help. But what could he do?

They sat there, thinking for a bit. Then Airavat had an

idea! He told Indra that he had seven trunks and divine powers too. He could help fill the clouds with water from the oceans and rivers. Indra looked up, his eyes shining with happiness.

"You think we can do that, Airavat?" he asked jovially.

"Of course! Anything for you," Airavat promised.

That's how they hatched the plan together. They would fill up clouds with water and send them across the world so that people could enjoy rains and use rainwater for farming and other activities.

Now if you're thinking that this is not how rain is formed, you are right. We all know the water cycle of evaporation and condensation that we've studied. But things like this do happen in the world of gods. And it's a cool story that uses this small seasonal aspect to entertain us. What's more, it also tells us that gods and their mounts are buddies who cannot see each other unhappy!

In the story, Airavat filled up his trunks with gallons of water and filled up cloud after cloud. Then the water was sent over as rain to the praying farmers. At first they were scared, then a little surprised. But the shock soon turned to happiness and joy and they began dancing in the drizzle. And up in the heavens, Airavat put Indra on his back and danced in joy at the happiness of the devotees.

Fun facts about Airavat:

- In one story, Airavat was cursed by Durvasa muni to lose all his divine powers and go back to the earth. He roamed as an ordinary wild elephant for a hundred years and returned to heaven only when he worshipped Shiv ji.
- Airavat was hiding under the ocean once, and Indra was unable to find him. He came out when the gods and demons churned the ocean for nectar.

Indra's mount is a mighty elephant. Here is a cute one for you to create and colour.

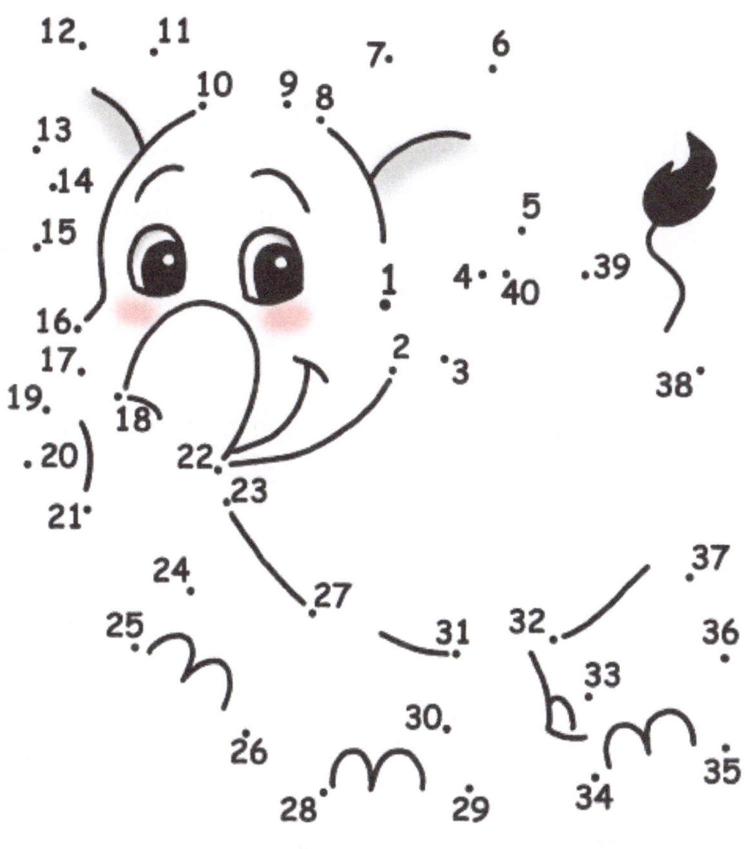

GANESHA
With his buddy Mushika-the mouse

- Son of Shiv ji and Parvati mata
- He loves laddus and eating, and is adoringly loved for his adventures

Abode: Kailash mountain.

Mount: Mushika, the mouse.

Weapons: Parashu (axe), Pash (noose).

You can recognize him due to:
Elephant head, he usually holds laddus and a lotus in his hands.

Festival: Ganesh Chaturthi

Consorts: Riddhi and Siddhi

Can a god ride a demon?

This story tells us how Ganesha, who is Shiv ji's son, ends up getting his mount because of one of Shiv ji's boons.

Gajamukhasura was a demon who was powerful and very proud. He believed he could defeat anyone in battle - whether it be gods or demons. Humans and animals could not even touch him, so he did not really worry about them.

In spite of having some super powers that nobody else could even think of, he was greedy for more. He decided to worship Shiv ji and ask for a boon. And what did he want? Like everyone else - immortality.

Do you know what immortality means? It means to live forever. (That is quite silly because everyone who is born has to die one day.) He was determined and performed penance for thousands of years to please Shiv ji.

Finally, the day came when Shiv ji appeared before him and offered him a boon. Gajamukhasura punched his fist in the air with happiness! He asked Shiv ji to bless him in such a way that he could never be killed with any weapon.

"Let no weapon in the whole wide world do me any harm," he bellowed in glee.

Shiv ji said, "Tathastu!" So be it, and it was done!

Shiv ji vanished after granting him the boon. Gajamukhasura swelled with pride, but started misusing his power soon after. He was a master of stealth and could also change his form. Using one trick or another, he fought with almost all the devas and rishis, spreading chaos wherever he went. Now everyone in all the three worlds became very scared of Gajamukhasura.

Gajamukhasura did not stop there. He was so full of pride that he went to swarga lok and defeated Indra, the king of gods.

Indra was driven out of his own home, and he was furious. He found out more about Gajamukhasura and went straight to Shiv ji.

"Bholenath! You have given so much power to a demon and now he is driving us all crazy. Why did you do this, oh all powerful god? Please help us. We all want to return to our home in heaven."

Shiv ji was a little surprised to know that Gajamukhasura was misusing his power and causing trouble. He had thought him to be a good fellow. Feeling guilty, he decided to help Indra and the other gods and rishis.

He realised that his son Ganesha could take care of the matter very well. He called Ganesha and asked him to help.

Little Ganesha was so happy that his father had given him an important task. Don't you also feel happy when your parents show confidence in you and tell you to do

something important? So Ganesha quickly got ready and set out to help Indra.

When he saw the demon breaking the ashram of some rishis, Ganesha got super angry. He decided to teach Gajamukhasura a lesson. He pulled out his bow and arrows and started aiming at the demon. But wait! What's this? Gajamukhasura started laughing!

The arrows were tickling him instead of injuring him. He began to laugh even harder.

Ganesha was very confused. Then he dug out his mace and charged at Gajamukhasura, but the blows of the mace felt like massage to the asura.

Ganesha tried all his other weapons one by one, but nothing happened to Gajamukhasura. Ganesha started getting worried. And why wouldn't he! He was a god, but this demon had his father's blessings. Ganesha had to think of something, and quickly!

Gajamukhasura charged at Ganesha to hit him, but Ganesha escaped. He started thinking of a plan. He had understood that this demon couldn't be killed using weapons. Then how?

"Idea!" he screamed, and pulled out one of his tusks. They were sharp as swords but they weren't any weapon. They were only the massive teeth of an elephant. It could definitely work.

As he threw the tusk at Gajamukhasura, the demon was taken by surprise. He decided to change into a mouse to save himself from the blow. But by then, the tusk had hit him in the chest. Gajamukhasura screamed in pain as he lay injured. Even in his pain, he prayed to Ganesha and asked for forgiveness. He promised that he would never bother anyone, and also be in Ganesha's service forever.

Ganesha accepted his apology and healed the demon, who had transformed into a mouse. He said that Gajamukhasura could stay with him. But how?

"Oh, would you like to be my vahana?" asked Ganesha. "You could take me places and also enjoy living with me on Mount Kailash. I think it will be great fun."

"It would be my honour," said Gajamukhasura with folded hands.

So, Ganesha named the mouse Mushika and took him along to Mount Kailash.

When I want to go somewhere, I first decide how I would go. Whether I'd take the metro, a bus or drive.

Similarly, when Ganesha has to go somewhere, he calls his favourite Mushika to take him to his destination.

Ever since, no matter where Ganesha has to go, the mouse is always with him. And since he is so small, he can take Ganesha to every nook and corner of the world. They have also become good friends now and have a lot of fun together.

Ganesha is invited for lunch

Whenever someone mentions Ganesha, the first word that comes to my mind is a laddu. Ganesha is very fond of food, especially sweets, and never lets go of a chance to feast.

Once, Kuber – the god of wealth – was visiting Mount Kailash. It was shining with snow-laden peaks and beautiful flora and fauna.

Being the god of wealth, Kuber was naturally very rich. He was very proud of the new city that he had built and wanted everyone to come and see his magnificent royal palace.

Shiv ji knew what Kuber was up to, so he and Parvati had not been accepting his invitations. This time, Kuber was adamant that he wouldn't go back without getting a 'yes' from them. "No matter what happens, this time Shiv ji won't be able to turn me down," he decided and set out to meet him.

He headed straight to Shiv ji and invited him again, insisting that he wouldn't leave till Shiv ji came with him. That put Bholenath in a fix. He wanted to say no, but didn't have the heart to disrespect a fellow god. So he found a simple way out. He called out to Ganesha and asked him to accompany Kuber to his new palace.

Shiv ji told Kuber, "King Kuber, I respect you and want to come with you, but I am occupied with an important task. I would love to send my son Ganesha with you."

Kuber wanted Shiv ji and Parvati mata to come with him, but how could he tell them that he wasn't happy to take only Ganesha? *What if Shiv ji got angry and cursed him. No, no! Let me take him and go, he thought.*

He told Shiv ji, "Prabhu, Ganesha is a child. I have made so much food for you and Parvati mata; that will all go waste! After all, how much can a child eat?"

Shiv ji smiled and assured him that nothing of the sort would happen. Ganesha was super excited to travel with Kuber uncle and visit his new palace. So he hopped on to his vahana Mushika, and left with Kuber.

When they reached the palace, Kuber respectfully seated Ganesha and Mushika in a beautiful room.

Then Kuber clapped twice and asked the servers to start serving the meal. Many attendants walked in, serving one dish after another. But Ganesha was happiest to see two big plates full of yummy laddus. He started eating slowly.

After a while, all the food in the room was in Ganesha's tummy, but he was still hungry. So a surprised Kuber ordered for more food to be brought in.

Again, a row of attendants got a fresh round of food for Ganesha. Soon enough, that was also finished.

This happened several times, after which the royal chef told Kuber that they had to begin cooking again, as all the food had been eaten up by the two guests. Kuber couldn't believe his ears!

But since there was nothing else they could do, the chefs cooked everything again. The servers served it again, and yet again, Ganesha quickly gobbled all of that too.

Now Kuber broke into a sweat, but he was too proud to show that he was worried. So he quickly brought in grains and food items from all over the city and had the cooks make the dishes all over again.

If something like this had happened today, we could have just ordered some food online! But we are talking of thousands of years back, you know. There were no food delivery apps back then!

All the food brought in this time too was gone in an hour.

Where? Into Ganesha's stomach, where else!

Now the food of the entire city had been cooked and served to Ganesha. The people of the city were standing outside Kuber's palace in confusion, wondering who this guest was. Kuber was standing outside the window of the room, confused and unable to think of a solution.

Finally, when Ganesha said he wanted more to eat, Kuber realised that this was all Ganesha's magic. He folded his hands in humility and apologised for being so proud. He had understood that Ganesha might be a baby, but the whole universe was a part of him. Kuber could not offer anything else to Ganesha, so he offered himself.

That pleased Ganesha. He thanked Kuber for his hospitality and took his leave.

As a parting gift, he magically replaced all the grains and food items in all houses of the city and the palace.

Fun facts about Ganesha:

- Ganesha devotees all over the world understand that if they have to call Ganesha to their house, they have to first welcome Mushika. So, during all festivities, especially during the Ganesha Chaturthi festival, Mushika is worshipped along with Ganesha.
- Devotees request Mushika to bring their beloved god Ganesha to their houses and bless their abode.

Isn't it amazing how a small mouse takes such a powerful, elephant-headed god to every nook and corner of the world!

KARTIKEYA
And his peacock-Parambani

- Son of Shiv ji and Parvati mata
- A warrior god, he is also the general of the army of gods

Abode: Kailash mountain, Palani Hills

Mount: Parambani, the peacock.

Weapons: Vel (spear)

You can recognize him due to:

Spear in his hands, he is seated on a peacock. His flag bears a rooster.

Festivals: Skanda Shashti, Kartik Purnima.

Consorts: Devasena and Valli

The Majestic Peacock for Kartikeya

Do you know who Kartikeya is? Well, he is the general of the army of the gods. He would lead the battles whenever a demon tried to create chaos. He has amazing powers, being the son of Parvati mata and Shiv ji. He is also Ganesha ji's elder brother.

He rides on a peacock and is considered to be one of the most adorable gods. But do you know how he came to have the peacock as his vahana? All thanks to his father. Let me tell you how!

Once there was a demon named Soorpadam. He was mighty powerful and wanted to be the king of all gods, demons and humans. He knew he could beat the humans and demons any day, but gods? Hmm, that would need some extra super powers.

So, he prayed to Shiv ji for a long time and appeased him with his dedication. Shiv ji came to Soorpadam and offered to grant him a boon for his tapasya. That's what the demon had been waiting for.

He quickly asked Shiv ji to make him the most powerful in the world. So powerful that the army of all the gods, even the master trickster Vishnu ji, could not defeat him.

Shiv ji was a little surprised with the wish, but then he thought – Soorpadam looks like a nice guy. He won't do anything evil. However, he did not know looks could be deceptive. So he said, "Tathastu!" and granted him the boon.

After that, Shiv ji went back to Mount Kailash. And Soorpadam went completely crazy, annoying everyone across the world.

The gods and humans were soon fed up of the evil doings of this demon. They went to Shiv ji. They complained and wanted to know the reason why Shiv ji had granted Soorpadam such a boon, making him almost invincible .

Shiv ji realised that he had perhaps made a mistake. He immediately thought of calling Vishnu ji for help. But oh! The boon safeguarded Soorpadam from Vishnu ji completely. Then who could beat him?

He thought and thought and thought. Finally he called his elder son Kartikeya.

Kartikeya heard what the devas had to say, and decided to end Soorpadam's evil doings forever.

He took up his weapons and went forth to fight with Soorpadam.

The battle went on for a long while. Kartikeya used his weapons one after another and tried to defeat the demon. Soorpadam, on the other hand, fought with all his might. When after a long and intense battle, he realised that he was unable to defeat Kartikeya, he started running.

Kartikeya gave chase to catch him! But Soorpadam was

a stealthy demon. He changed himself into a mango tree and stood still. Was it like playing hide and seek? Did he think a god won't be able to see what he was up to? How silly!

Soorpadam thought he was being very smart, and was sure Kartikeya would never find him.

On the other hand, Kartikeya recognised Soorpadam in the form of the tree as soon as he saw it. But he was intelligent, so he pretended to not have noticed him.

When Soorpadam relaxed, Kartikeya turned around and threw his mighty spear at the tree. The throw was so strong that it pierced the tree, and cut the trunk into two pieces. Soorpadam had been caught!

When the tree was attacked, from one side of the tree flew out a peacock, and from the other end flew out a rooster.

Cockadoodledooooo!

Such was the power of Kartikeya, that all the evil of Soorpadam was destroyed. What remained was only the goodness. The two birds bowed their heads and did pranam to Kartikeya.

They offered themselves in his service. Kartikeya made the peacock his mount, and the rooster took its place on the flag on Kartikeya's chariot, announcing his arrival wherever the brave god went.

That is how Parambani the peacock ended up being the vahana of the war god Kartikeya.

Race with his brother, Ganesha

Kartikeya and Parambani have had a lot of adventures together. The god is never seen without the peacock by his side. They have become the best of friends, since they spend so much time together.

In fact, Parambani is also friends with Ganesha's mount - Mushika, the mouse. That wasn't always the case. There was a time when Parambani thought he was more beautiful and the mouse was not very good looking. But as time passed, the peacock realised that there were many things that he couldn't do that the mouse could.

They became great friends after the race between Ganesha and Kartikeya.

Let me tell you about this interesting race.

As you already know, Shiv ji lives with his family on Kailash mountain. So one day, on a particularly sunny day on the cold snow-covered mountain, the family was sitting together and chit-chatting. It was like a weekend for the gods.

Parvati mata had made laddus for little Ganesha, and he

was busy gulping them down. Kartikeya was also enjoying the sweets when Ganesha whispered to him, "You know bhaiya, Maa loves me more. That's why she has made laddus for me."

Kartikeya knew laddus were Ganesha's favourite food, but he also knew that his parents loved both of them equally.

I have often teased my younger brother in the same way, but he used to start crying. The little cry baby! He should have known, that no matter what someone says to you, parents can never discriminate between their children. They love them all the same.

Kartikeya was cool; he laughed.

But Ganesha didn't stop there, and went on teasing. That's the moment when the notorious Narad muni appeared. He joined the fun and asked Kartikeya and Ganesha what the discussion was about.

When he came to know how Ganesha had been teasing Kartikeya, he suggested both of them to have a race. Whoever completed the round of the world first and came back to Kailash, would be the winner.

Kartikeya laughed, knowing that his peacock would be faster than the mouse any day. So he agreed. Ganesha, on the other hand, knew too well that there was a slim chance of him winning the race. He had to think of a plan. So, he asked Narad muni, "Sire, can you tell me again what the race is about?"

"Of course, little one! Whoever takes a full round of the world and comes back to where I am standing, will be the winner of the race."

The boys agreed and got ready.

Narad muni was the referee, so he said, "On your mark, get set, go!"

At the word 'go', Kartikeya swished past everyone and flew up!

But where was Ganesha?

He was smiling, sitting right where he was!

He took a round of his parents and said out loud, "My parents are my world. I don't need to go anywhere to find the world."

Everyone was impressed with his wisdom and how intelligently he had understood the riddle.

When Kartikeya got back, he was confused at how Ganesha had reached first. But then, Ganesha offered Kartikeya his favourite rice meal, and Mushika gave Parambani some seeds and water because they had travelled so far.

Then the family and Narad muni sat together and had a good feast! Everyone laughed as Kartikeya twisted little Ganesha's big ears, laughing. Remember, a family that eats together, spends quality time together, is a strong family.

Fun facts about Kartikeya:

- Parambani is shown as holding a snake in its talons. The snake symbolises ego, and it shows the need to control one's ego.
- Kartikeya is celebrated as one of the most good looking and handsome gods.

Let us know our gods better!

Across

2. Weapon of the king of gods
5. The prime weapon used by Shiv ji
7. Vishnu's vahana
9. The demon that Durga maa killed after a 9-day long battle
11. A snow white elephant with four tusks
12. The sweet that Ganesh ji loves the most

Down

1. Shiv ji's wife
3. Vehicle shared by God of creation and Goddess of wisdom
4. Lakshmi ji travels on this bird
6. The bird that sits on Kartikeya's chariot flag
8. A black cat is the vahana of this goddess
10. The bull who is the head of all Shiva ganas

SHITALA MATA

- An incarnation of Parvati mata
- She is the goddess of coolness, who is known to fight illnesses and fever

Mount: Donkey

Weapons: Broom, hand fan, water pot.

You can recognize her due to:

The broom in hand, seated on a donkey.

Festival: Shitala Ashtami

Consort: Jvarasura

SHANI DEV

- Personification of planet Saturn
- Born to Surya (Sun god) and Chhaya
- Considered an important part of Hindu astrology
- Controller of age, misery, pain, sorrow, ambition, discipline, old age, among others

Abode: Shani lok

Mount: Crow

Weapons: Sceptre, trident, axe.

You can recognize him due to:

Dark complexion, sceptre in his hand, seated on a crow.

Festivals: Shani Jayanti, worshipped on Saturdays.

Consorts: Manda and Neelima.

YAMA DEV

- God of death and justice, he was born to Surya and Sanjna
- He is believed to keep a tab on people's karma and assign them their rightful place after death
- He is the protector of the southern direction

Abode: Yama lok

Mount: Buffalo

Weapons: Danda (sword), Noose, Mace.

You can recognize him due to:

Dark complexion, riding a buffalo.

Consort: Dhumorna

GANGA

- The river Ganges, best known for purity and forgiveness
- She is considered to be Parvati mata's sister
- Ganga rests in Shiv ji's hair

Abode: Settled in Shiv ji's hair, Brahma lok.

Mount: Makar (crocodile)

Weapon: Kalash (metal pot)

Festivals: Ganga Dussehra, Ganga Jayanti.

Consort: Shantanu

GODDESS YAMUNA

- Yamuna is considered to be Yama dev's twin sister, born to Surya and Sanjna
- Plays an important role in the early life of Krishna – Vishnu ji's avatar

Abode: Surya lok, Yamunotri.

Mount: Tortoise

You can recognize her due to:

Sitting on a tortoise, holding a water pot in her hand.

Festival: Yamuna Jayanti

Consort: Krishna

A note of thanks

Just like all good things must be concluded with gratitude, I am ending this book with a note of thanks to all those who have made this book possible.

The Srishti Publishers family, my second home. They patiently and lovingly nudge me every time I slow down. Special thanks to Bose sir, Arup and Vijay ji.

Super talented illustrator Ishan Trivedi, whose illustrations brought my stories to life. Thanks, Ishan.

The lively designer friend, Sugandha Jule Bedi; she made sure the illustrations and words came together to create magic.

Special shout out to Pushpanjali, who edited the raw draft. Her inputs were valuable and very helpful.

Never forgetting the love and immense affection my readers shower on me.

And forever thankful to god for blessing me with a family that inspires me to get better with each day. My parents by birth, love and law have pampered me immensely.

My bhabis - Niharika, Akshima and Swati – helped me proofread the book at such a short notice. They make me believe in love.

Saving the best for the end – My husband, Vipul and my son, Amay. You are my heart, and my soul.

Thank you Yajas and Khushee, for multiplying my motherly affection.

A big thanks to all of you!